Praise for
Language of the Wound is Love

In *Language of the Wound is Love,* Megha Sood amplifies a constancy of the past within a shifting sense of place and thirst for belonging. Throughout this gutsy, incandescent collection, Sood often investigates quandaries of thought within the physical self: *our tongue moves in a way our body can't decipher in grief.* Her intimate grief and fury mirror our collective bewilderment, while nonetheless evoking a stubborn tenderness for the world— *I can still feel the hallowed existence of everything around me*—and redemption: *my granny combing my hair and making trails of kindness.* From one line to the next, these poems shiver against each other like ripples of memory across time.

—**Stephanie JT Russell,** Dutchess County Poet Laureate, author of
One Flash of Lightning: A Samurai Path for Living the Moment

Megha Sood's moving new poetry collection, *Language of the Wound is Love* eloquently conveys the depths of grief frequently experienced by immigrants of color in the US due to the dominant culture rarely allowing them to truly feel at home as they endeavor to create lives here. The ineluctable pain that comes with never truly belonging thrums throughout, and Sood deftly conveys how rejecting, dehumanizing, and isolating "the other" is not only cruel, it's illogical. For what are people at their core, but souls? The beautiful, shining soul has no color, no ethnicity. It knows no barriers. These elegant, sophisticated poems engender empathy as they remind us to look past what makes one an outsider and embrace the being inside. Find your humanity. See yourself. It's a beautiful book.

—**Toni Ann Johnson,** Flannery O'Connor award-winning author
of *Light Skin Gone to Waste*

Megha Sood has outdone herself as a poet in her latest collection, *Language of the Wound is Love*. Her language is expansive, stretched to hold the unfolding personal and global suffering and offer us a reprieve in the poet's imagination. These are poems of longing, desiring to set the world right.

—**Pramila Venkateswaran,** Suffolk County Poet Laureate,
author of *We are Not a Museum*

Megha Sood is no stranger to the terror of hunger. And what poet has not felt the hunger of a poem? Rather than be diminished by it, Sood is propelled to write aloud, adopt a language of her own to face contradictions, and be a faithful witness to the real world. This knowledge is her salvation as she finds home in the *attar*-perfumed folds of her clothes, and her henna and turmeric-tainted fingers.

—**Maria Lisella,** author of *Thieves in the Family*,
Academy of American Poets Laureate Fellow

We must support each other and empathize with each other, wrote Maya Angelou because each of us is more alike than we are unalike; poet and literary activist Megha Sood writes into such expansive abstractions of love, belonging, hope, migration, and grief with enviable sincerity. At her finest, as in the poem "Deciphering the Madness, the thick rope of time goes through the wide-open mouth of a blind wall while garbage trucks ping and finches weave nests in the oak. Sood uses her platform admirably to advocate for equity and social justice.

—**Dr. Ravi Shankar,** Pushcart Prize-winning author of 17 books

Language of the Wound Is Love is a deeply personal journey through the physical and emotional wounds in the process of healing. The poet's storytelling is strong with its vulnerable turn of phrase and connection from one piece to another. Once I started, I couldn't put it down until the final outreach to hope.

—**RescuePoetix | Susan Justiniano,** Poet, Author,
Spoken Word Artist, Playwright, Advocate

There is an urgency to these poems written while bombs fall, emotional axes swirl, and dilemmas sear. Sood addresses essential questions. What happens when one immigrates? How to live while your brother and sister are being slaughtered elsewhere on this one earth? Yes, the wound is love, suppurating, challenging, insisting on its poetry, and the healing that comes from bloodletting.

—**Indran Amirthanayagam,** author of *Seer*

Language of the Wound is Love

A Collection of Poems

FLOWERSONG
PRESS

Megha Sood

FLOWERSONG
PRESS

FlowerSong Press
Copyright © 2025 by Megha Sood
ISBN: 978-1-963245-96-7

Published by FlowerSong Press
in the United States of America.
www.flowersongpress.com

Edited by Candice Louisa Daquin

Image Credit:
Ryunosuke Kikuno via Unsplash.com

Set in Adobe Garamond Pro

NOTICE: SCHOOLS AND BUSINESSES
FlowerSong Press offers copies of this book at quantity discount with bulk purchase for educational, business, or sales promotional use. For information, please email the Publisher at info@flowersongpress.com.

For Siddharth

table of contents

(II) Language of the Wound is Love

(III) Every Pain Has a Story

(IV) The Collective State of Disbelief

(V) Brotherhood

"Be kind, for everyone you meet
is fighting a harder battle."

–Plato

Language of the Wound is Love

A Collection of Poems

Poem and Its Hunger

Do you ever realize how the body reclaims itself?
Like the dried scar from its time of birth.

You only realize its presence when you see it.
Hunger reeks from your soul,

and like water from a mother's hair wrung after a bath,
it brings out scented memories of something
pure and sublime.

We all enter a poem knowing its hunger and emerge
stripped naked of our emotions.

There is always a death standing at the end of the sentence,
not every enjambment gives meaning.

Some lines are meant to be left orphaned. Like the day they found
an old crumpled picture of my bombed city in my wallet.

We all enter a poem knowing its hunger. Like a night feverishly trying to
find its salvation in the open mouth of the bloody dawn.

(I)

Language Lost

My Identity as a First-Generation Immigrant

Empathy stems from the mouth of love, of hunger, of acceptance
an incessant desire to be known as a countryman in a town full of

wonders. A land of opportunity as told by toothy-grinned ancestors.
I hear your wails in the thicket of night, heat rising through my spine,

leaving my walnut skin pocked with welts and blisters—another day of spineless crime.
Little difference does language make if the heart is emptied of compassion—

Protection takes a different meaning when the protectors start to devour.
I curl my words as your name slips and falls off my tongue.

Like a sin in this country, built on borrowed hopes and desires,
crouched and shriveled, shrinking our existence a little bit more, every time.

Treading narrow streets filled with slurs resting on forked tongues and
bent spines, carrying silver-etched dreams of my ancestors with

throats laced with parables of truth. Soft hands with sweet bay leaf
fragrance, holding a sepia-tinged tattered book, carrying the love for generations.

My identity carved as a first-generation immigrant in a land built
on the calloused hands that are painted with silvery dreams of kingdoms to come.

How to Save a Child Fleeing War?

Based on the fact that; "More than 10.5 million people have been displaced by the war in Ukraine. That number includes 4 million who have fled abroad, half of whom are children."

—The Wall Street Journal, May 12, 2022

i

Open your palms and hold gently
as if you are nursing a wounded bird left astray.
Look for places where a soul has been scarred
those deep ravines of grief slowly making their way.

ii

Gently inspect each layer of their existence,
as it has been shattered and ripped in places.
Look for scathed memories that have been fissured
seeking acceptance for a soul lost astray.

iii

Wipe their face pitted with streaming tears
as they make thin sluices–
for pain deeply carved in their heart
madly hoping for another brighter day.

iv

Unburden their soft shoulders
carrying remnants of a bombed house,
a last toy, and a crumpled family picture
they could barely save.

v

Try to lessen the ache of standing
over a mother's grave, a day before,
which left them with the inability to voice any pain.

vi

Gently wash their grief of losing a definition of home
being branded a refugee in a span of a single day.
Comfort those soft feeble feet carrying anguish
of a thousand bleeding hearts looking for solace in a stranger's embrace.

vii

Make sure there is no sudden noise, as minds of grief and terror
get triggered in innumerable ways. Refrain from asking questions
about leaving in the middle of the night, to an unknown place.

viii

Make sure to shower endless love and comfort
on this innocent soul whose life is paying the price
of a senseless war conceived in the devious minds
of tyrants and their greed-stricken ways.

ix

Don't take them back to the streets
laced with the dead bodies of their loved ones
and their home now turned
into a place of pitted mass graves.

x

Try to teach the lesson of our faceless humanity
this world has to offer to a five-year-old orphan
holding a crumpled photo of their family,
in their soft supple hands, refusing to give it away.

Deciphering the Madness

I ask the night, feverishly
as it rests on the caliginous back of time
like a thick rope going through
the wide-open mouth of a blind wall
rubbing against it, leaving marks on its existence.

Like a divine mark on the forehead
after kneeling before exalted Gods
countless times.

I ask myself.

Is it ever going to be alright again?

Thinking, as I take a second glance
at the empty streets of my house
longing for the clickety-clack of footsteps
warming its thick cobbled skin.

There is a method to this madness
that I used to discover—
every morning looking outside my window
counting hurried whispers of crowds
as they move towards the station like a mass exodus.

Now I long for those sights I normally abhorred
the state of normalcy of what it was before
as the light sheepishly makes its way
through thin wooden slats of my bedroom window.

Is it ever going to be alright again?

The pinging sound of the garbage truck
backing up in an alley,
soft paws scratching as they dig through dirt
in the almost bald spot of the park
joggers clad in sweaty bodies
heaving to take in another sliver of breath.

Is it ever going to be alright again?

I look at tiny finches weaving a nest in the oak
tree outside my apartment,
as they decipher this reigning madness
carefree weaving home for their future self.

I say to myself,
It is indeed going to be alright again.

Born on the Other Side of Hate

Love   like a sacred offering
a frail feather with its filigree ends,
Love   like a last kiss
an almost forgotten memory—
scribbled on the sweaty forehead of her son.

Her heart distended as the night takes
one more soul to consume the darkness,
her desire desiccated in the summer sun
crow's feet engraving a lifelong suffrage.

Pain deeply carved on her skin
time spitting it out in pieces and shards
she sits calmly, gently caressing golden locks
on the forehead of her sleeping son.

Her voice trembling with fear
of her last haunted memory,
the unknown voice on the other side
of the door jammed by her frail belongings.

Her lullabies have to fight tooth and nail
through her fears and anxiety,
though every bit of her soul is on fire
she morphs that rage with soothing apricity.

Undulating breaths as they touch
her warm heaving bosom,
she clutches her body together
giving a warm ambrosial embrace,
to the one she loves—
to the one who was born
in a peaceful country
born on the   other side of hate.

Ten Ways of Looking at Hunger

I

Stars dazzle in the ashen sky on a cold night streaming and making long traces of hopes bouncing from one end to another, tracing a path for you to place your wish. A wish is hunger in its infancy.

II

A simmering passion rises from the dearth of your acceptance, birthing at the corners of your mouth. Lingering desire scorched by societal norms and you wait to exist in a different dimension. The language of the wound is love.

III

A cold gaze on the morning of the funeral waits to gulp down the memories, as you bury the remnants of your happiness in a warm womb of trowled earth, whose skin is broken by the lash of overnight rains. Acceptance is a fallacy.

IV

An incessant desire to look for the likeness of the soul, as your identity sits like a square knob in the circular opening of this godforsaken life, and your identity is solely defined by what lies between your soft supple thighs. Love is an elegy for acceptance.

V

An uninterrupted clacking of soft beaks, as it waits for the next morsel, pushed down its supple throat as fledglings make their home in the oak tree in my courtyard and I think of a thousand ways to call their hunger my own.

VI

A desire for survival as the frail scorched hands of a child hold the photo of their bombed city, carrying the identity of a refugee, looking for a stranger's embrace. A single night demarcates your identity.

VII

Searching for a definition of elusive peace, as he breaks another morsel from the dried rye bread making a constellation around his courtyard, giving sustenance to the gray-winged visitors flocking his courtyard. A lame excuse to fill the emptiness in his weary old heart.

VIII

A life nothing but a deluge of expectations, waiting to jump across the gushing terrain, in a race for survival, spawning only to meet death in a run for life. A shimming desire in the cold white eye of a salmon.

IX

An unsung, unfinished lullaby that will haunt their existence forever, as they decide on the color of the coffin matching the dress of her doll, thinking of ways to bring that last phantom smile to her face.

X

Hunger speaks in thousands of ways, in a language unknown to many, and yet cleaves a soul asking for more. Making thin sluices of suffering, desire, and loneliness, scratching a path in our existence to carry pain. A flute carved deep to sustain melody.

Permanence

Nothing is permanent *says the leaves*
interred in the drenched gardens of my puny home.

Embraced by the sustenance of moist earth
crumbled and soaked in the fragrance of the petrichor.

Thick cumulus straddling through open skies tasting their blue kindness.
Love is transient. We all are travelers seeking a home in the midst of a storm.

Stripped from the mighty boughs of Oak, leaves have learned their lessons.
Lulled to sleep in the heaving bosom of the ashen night.

Acceptance is just a fallacy. A truth deeply etched in sullen memories
of those who arrived before.

We fall. We all will fall.

Waiting for the divine moment to arrive.
No one finds *home* ever. No matter how deep you root.

Ghost in a Different Dimension

Musings during my housewarming in the United States

Countless names sit orphaned around the circle of fire in my *havan kund*
during the ritual at my housewarming, engulfing every definition of home

that I hold close to my heart. My tongue frenziedly tries to mold and morph
every syllable in this foreign land. My spindly legs dangle continuously to get a foothold,

an unnamed longing, to find the portion of land under my feet every morning.
A feverish desire to bring back the ethereal taste of my country.

A remembrance that I create annually during my festivals without fail.
The endless depth of this longing disgusts me sometimes.

This fruitless desire of a dandelion to find rooting somewhere, anywhere—
Trying passionately to keep alive the fragrance of my mother's turmeric-laced recipes,

to seep deeply into the thin dry walls of my high-rise apartment
that sits next to a river flowing unfettered, between its two longing ends.

Reminding me endlessly that it was not this dream that swirled in my wide eyes
when I began my journey in this naked nation, with its dark humor.

The nation that celebrates my new beginnings by smearing streets with the blood of
my brothers and sisters. The feeling that scrapes identity from the skin of my tongue

and scratches clean warm-colored henna from my soft hands when asked every time
in the cold streets by unnamed voices, to go back to where I belong.

*Legends: Havan Kund: It is the center place in which the fire is put on, and all the
offerings are made during a Hindu religious ceremony.*

Love is Nothing but an Elegy for Acceptance

We all long for a fairy tale sequinned with a kind-hearted prince or princess
an enchanted alchemist—
brimming with love and passion,
magically turning our sparking dreams into pure gold.
We all dream, eyes open wide, while growing in our soft porous bodies,
ready for those tender dreams to take hold.

When our desires are judged by the sex
that rests between our supple thighs.
A fervent desire for acceptance with hunger—
when our existence cannot be validated,
beyond the binary and everything else is damned.

Your name sits like a sin on my tongue
in this socially demarcated society
living by cookie-cutter rules.
My desires frayed and bleeding at the ends
trying to fit hard within the mold.

Love is nothing but an elegy for acceptance.

And yet I stand here, waiting for my own,
at the crossroads of life, judging me.
I with knees pressed against concrete in a church pew
apologizing for my frail existence.

With soil dowsed by the tears of our existence,
tears of our survival—
I always wrap the color of my wound around my heart
as it catches shine from a kind sun.

Love was always folklore to me; a soothing lullaby,
a hushed prayer, told by my granny,
as she bravely witnessed the pain of generations jumping hoops.

Living life is nothing but a farce,
a menagerie of corrugated desires,
though I stayed put.

When the choices of my life were foreshowed
by my jagged heart and cold shoulders,
I always ran blinded by my sense of false comfort.

Flash forward, and here I am standing tall and proud like an old oak
in the numbness of night—
as a witness to my years of survival.

Trying to scrape the knife wounds
on my thick skin made by ignorant hands.

Those hands, swelling with the pride of false ownership.

Just Another Day, Just Another Rape

Based on the Hathrus Gangrape in India, September 2020

Body mutilated, eyes scourged, throat strangled
cut and slashed, the body bears suppurating marks
welts and blisters, wounds of caste inequality
the penultimate sin of being born into a low-caste family
where simple touch is shunned by society.

A body so impure, even the shadow it bears
like a scavenger, has been pulled and slashed to shreds
as she fights her battle of being born in a nation
that stands mute and dumb to the atrocities.

To millions of daughters before and countless after her
dragged and burned on pyres to prove their marriage loyalty
a shaved head and simple living conforms
love toward her departed husband,
whose death is a fault of hers to repent.

Where the upper caste rules this nation with an iron fist
as they lay lien to her soul,
scavenging identity and mutilating her
hasn't been enough for them, I guess anymore.

Burned and cremated in fires,
the nakedness of this nation spills
through the empty eyes of a billion souls,
as they scroll through the news on their phones
another rape, another news.

Stripped of her dignity, devoid of the privilege
of being cremated with last rites is too much to ask for,

in this nation that stands dumb and mute
another hamster on the wheel routine—
another strip of news to abhor.

Streets lined with wails and cries of mothers
losing their daughters in dim-lit streets, in fields
in a thicket of night, in the brightness of day.
Yet their soul-numbing cries fail to reach privileged ears
holding lien to the amicable society
led by the scriptures, as they claim.

These streets are now laced with incessant wails and sobs
only to find them gutted and stripped of their dignity
brimming with the pain of mothers whose tears are dried up.
An act in vain, an exercise in futility.

Gaping mouth like a toothless animal
devoid of any defense, bear witness to this atrocity
when another daughter becomes an offering
like a sacrificial lamb to this exalted society.

A society, that bootstraps itself, after falling from grace
every damn time and gets ready for the next day
to read another ravenous killing of their *betis*
as just another scroll on their phone
a nation's favorite pastime.

Legends: *Betis: Daughters*

Deserted

On the checkered path of life
a life so vain and unpredictable—
she stands there as a witness to injustice

a sharp blow to her convictions
at the crossroads of her uncertain life
reflecting a blind soliloquy in her numb mind

fighting all the incongruous thoughts
in her former pragmatic mind
that once knew all the answers
a mind now devoid of any explanation

muted mind unable to grasp any meaning
those merciless scratches, she often finds
on her glass window,

"Go back to where you belong"

unable to fathom such mindless cruelty
and disgust, she asks her heart
again and again, with no response

fervently looking for forgotten answers
to the one and the only question;
where does one belong,
when the only home you ever knew, deserts you?

I Have Called Many Places Home

as my shelter, my refuge,
solace to my wandering soul,
a place to seek peace from lingering doom
that nourishes my taloned fingers and crestfallen soul.

I have called many places home
a place where peace is woven
in lingering shadows on walls
a singular point of existence—
that starts to make sense once and for all.

The place of continuity
a streak of life in the underbelly of autumn leaves
an old Chestnut tree as it boisterously stands
in the courtyard,
providing solace and comfort to thee.

I have called many places home
where the scorched earth goes green,
where the serenity seeps into your soul
and the soul comes alive once more.

I have called many places home.
I have *yet* to make one though.

Provenance of My Rage

A sudden gush of emotions
slowly traverses—
rising like scorched mercury
through the knots of my undulating spine.

An unsettling notion of standing
a little too close to the kiln
my emotions rise and reach a crescendo
simmering and brimming to the core.

Words are failing to form in my mouth
falling incessantly to their untimely death
mumbling and gnashing teeth—
spitting truth in between.

Here the veracity of my truth depends
on the color of my skin
and the exalted Gods in heaven
to those, I pray with my folded hands.

This unsettling feeling of fear and nameless rage
I feel under my walnut skin,
as I walk on the empty streets in the morning
fighting the loneliness and voiceless din.

Confronted by a stranger's voice
that sends shivers to my bone;
laced with privilege, passed to him for generations
with his blue blood coursing through his veins.

A country he boisterously calls *home*
asking me with the sheer audacity
of his forked tongue in his vile voice,
hurling insults wrapped in his privilege
to go back,
to where I belong.

House of Our Forgotten Past

I mourn the shadows
those misty monsters—
clad in the nostalgia
in the mosaic of our inner integument

taking a pound of flesh
for every time I go down that path
trodden with spikes of pointy memories

gnawing at my solace
there is always resistance
hesitation,
a slight glitch,
in wiping out that dust

slow darkening of the window sill
time blackens everything—
with that thin film of powdered dust
of my pulverized dreams

as cobwebs get thick
and windows get dusty,
those warm magnolias
dying again in my pink vase

memories stripping off
the chipped walls
peeling off gracefully
and nails getting rusty
in the house of our forgotten past.

Branded

His words slashed the air into halves
catching remnants of his tradition in his cupped palms
carrying the taste of his legacy,
on the thin skin of his tongue
pain knotted in the arch of his spine.

He rises through the air
suffused with the lost translation of his misused language
always seen as a threat in this new world,
a clarion call mispronounced so far—
the atrocities carved on the blistered skin
of his sons and daughters.

He rises to violently claim the freedom that was truly his
a taste he deprived his ashen soul of for eons
an almost forgotten luxury—
fleeting his age, he so fervently desires.

What good is a place if it lacks the definition of a home?

The twinkle in the eyes of his newborn
was sacred as a muezzin call to prayer.
pure and serene—
He knew that his home meant
more than the square piece of parched barren land
that has birthed nothing but empty promises.

Like the dried eyes of his aging father
as he returns empty-handed every day
whitened by the heat of the unkind sun.

His calloused hands bearing the whips
of the unrelenting time
his back bent and arched
failing to call the piece of land his home
salvation for the marred souls;
in the country
branding him a refugee
for times unknown.

Futile

Bellowing down the corridors of time, reverberating with the sensibility of a wounded artist. Torn at the heart, emotions splayed out and frayed at the seams, ready to burst apart. What more can happen in these moments of vulnerability where everything lies at the opening of the mouth of hunger, of endless desires, of resonating pain? We are exposed to the deepest form of our fears, standing at the intersection of wants, ready to face the slanting mawed transgressions in life. We all know that hunger pierces a man the most and yet we stand against each other, with our drooping shoulders, with pulverized hopes, ready to crumble into a million pieces with the slight touch of a finger. One can spell out the hunger of humanity more clearly than the cold body of an immigrant child with a swollen abdomen, stuffed with hate. Screaming at both ends of the border, laying futile claims to the pieces of land that never belonged to him. *Come*, press your ear to the throbbing heart of Gaia, and listen to the pulsating pain she carries in her womb intermixed with screeches. The never-ending wails that fill the air with pain resonate for years to come. That soft lullaby is spoken as sacred prayers in the ears of a newborn that without fail turns into a war cry. You stand here dumb and mute, looking closely at your borders sealed with the flesh of your loved ones and moist earth seeped with the blood of those you once loved.

An Elegy is a Gesture Toward Acceptance

Grief curdles up like an overnight bowl of milk
left on my marbled kitchen countertop.

I want my sullen memories scraped and unsullied of their painful reminders.
Pristine and clean like the serrated edge of a butcher's knife.

Those remnants of life swirling around my eyes
morphing and molding images, like fluffy cumulus in cerulean skies.

Art conjured out of thin air, clinging to the belief of stardust
in our pores, ultimately forming a perfect concoction.

An elixir for life. They call it art. An act of forming
images out of soft pockets of vapor in the sky, a beautiful gift.

Here in this moment confounded by death, grief grazes my tongue
with pain slithering on the thin skin, unable to form a syllable.

I stand here with my knotted language, in a room filled with strangers
grazed by the same moment. With my feet, a plinth of the broken earth.

I stand looking at the calm closed eyelids of my dead father
soft light piercing through his supple skin still carries warmth.

Unable to form a legible sentence, my language has lost
its soul in his gaping mouth, a blind cave of pain.

Here, I stand alone again at the intersection of a moment
waiting for the grief to rise and curdle up.

Unable to offer elegy as an acceptance
on an empty funeral morning.

Language Lost

I twist and turn my supple tongue
words forming on its thin skin—

To pronounce your name in this world
full of desires, full of fear, full of hunger.

The edges of my mouth curl into sin
by those who mispronounce my love
into an unknown fear.

They call it a threat—

I call out your name in the dark
incessantly,
but my words fail me.

Every damn time.

Like the day I saw your
cinder ash-gray body
pulled out of that dark cold river.

Its coldness traveled the back of my frozen spine
raising every single hair on the back of my neck.

The moment rend me into a million pieces.
Grief as thick rounded black stones
sitting atop my throbbing chest.

And just like that cold winter morning
on a funeral day,
I lost my words.
Again.

(II)

Language of the Wound is Love

Topography of a Wound

What is the topography of a wound?

The origin and provenance of its existence
and its presence defined by its gaping mouth
by the broken semantics of love, hunger, and acceptance.

An old haggard face trying to find its identity
in a shattered mirror to salvage the possibility
of finding its crochet voices in haunting
broken cold corridors of life.

What is a vernacular of pain?

When it screams, haunts, and rattles
us in the night
trying to find flesh lodged
between its saw-edged teeth.

A ghostly presence—
This scar, this wound, has deeply etched in our souls
its haunting melody like a protracted fog in winter
bouncing off thickened concrete.
like a bullet ricocheting in the dark,
like a faint voice in the shroud of the night.

An elegy is an acceptance of the truth—
A black body in the middle of a protest
bare naked with arms splayed
pinned like a monarch
ready for the dumb menageries.

Another news making the headline
for its mindless span of a news cycle.
Prey ready to be devoured
trying to find that sliver of empathy
in the white of your eyes.
Pinning knees on the harsh concrete
as it makes deep impressions
into the hollowed past of this country
asking a bowlful of questions
in its bleary eyes.

A question laced with a deep hunger and empathy
a hunger that rises in my throat,
panic throbbing like a taut wire
devoid of its symphony.

Fear courses in my deep black veins
as the thick blue knees are pressed
a little harder than the last time.

Planting Seeds in a Detention Center

Immigration and Customs Enforcement held 32,743 in ICE detention according to data currently as of August 27, 2023. 66.1% held in ICE detention have no criminal record, according to data currently as of August 27, 2023. Many more have only minor offenses, including traffic violations. - Source: TRAC Immigration

Time drags its heavy steps like death:
its presence felt on my brittle ribcage
as my raspy breath makes another failed attempt
to leave this gilded cage.

Time, like the promise of a lover,
always brimming with hope,
yet ready to deceive you in the blink of an eye
makes its presence felt on my fingertips
as I make another scratch on the wall to anoint this day.

Hope comes like a faint lingering scent
of home-cooked food.

Memory is the name of the wound.
I relive each passing day.
Grief thick as stone sits atop my chest
and tries to break every syllable of love
that I hold softly in the folds of my tongue.

As I dream of tracing the poem on your curves
an undulating symphony I passionately desire.
But here I sit alone, quietly in this room
like a raisin soaked with the emptiness of time
swelling like a wound—
opening my mouth to yet another transgression.

As they stuff the syllables of language and demarcation
trying to mold and morph my body
that has been dragged across invisible lines in the ground
throat parched by the ignorance of those,
who once offered their soft cushions to our lullabies,
have now built shiny cages for my newborn.

The language of my ancestors
is now a rib cage symphony
trying to make a home through barbed wires
carving deep scratches on my walnut skin
trapped on the other side of this town.

Like the sparrows robbed of their shadows
to the evening sun, I genuflect,
soft knees making an impression in the soil.

Once crumbled by the thick calloused fingers of my father
as he laid the seeds into the broken soil
Mother never discriminates, he always said.
it gives back bountifully.

I remember this and more
as I look at the seeds giving back the bounty
breaking and growing through the pain,
around my walled cage.

My Bones Rattle with Crimson Rage

The sharp wind
grazes my tongue
like your disagreement with
how I live my life
your pointy misconceptions
about how it has been traded for things
to give you little pleasures
at the expense of my happiness
an exercise in vain

the black metallic taste
my unspoken truths
sit at the back of my throat
mulling in obsidian time
resting precariously on my forked tongue
slithering and infusing that deep
sense of fear in the roots of your hair
as they stand on the back of your neck

I fear the day my shredded truth
will drip and taint your soul
your pristine soul,
and your rambunctious gesture of owning everything
will crumble like a house of cards
in your phony wonderland

Your ramshackle leash around my neck
hasn't choked me enough
to knock the wind
out of my chest
those broken rods

though pounded a million times
by your sheer ignorance
hasn't given in yet

You,
with a smirk on your face
think I have caged my heart
but I have given it armor
against your vulture beak
as it tries to pry the truth from me

My bones rattle in a symphony
with crimson rage
This body is mine.
This body is not an apology.

Time's Up

Based on the appalling behavior of Donald Trump during his four toxic years of presidency

Stuck in this state of a purgatorial chasm
sitting between the rim of dreams and pungent reality
we are witnesses to the unknown future
to avoid or to ignore—
has become our constant fatality.

Truth and lies dangling like a filigree thread
of justice, we hold in high power,
a sad reflection of the dichotomy of our lives
we are dealing with our eyes wide shut
awaiting a monster ready to devour.

Our destiny is in the hands of a mendacious president
who rules with an iron fist
seething with greed and lust,
the abomination of holding a lien on everyone's life
and playing it like a sin.

When all you are left in your heart
are stories of disgrace and disagreements
ripping the nation alive
birthing monstrous divisiveness.

Where the truth, a matter of discussion, has turned sour
facts are mirrored as impotent and vile
lies you spread have come back to haunt you
like a dirty swarm of flies.

Your shameless smirk makes us gag and throw our heads back in shame
when innocent souls are locked up in cages
unborn babies scrubbed from mothers
with their hands tied in the back.

How do you justify the sanctity of this nation
when the protectors start to devour?
When sidewalks of this nation
are laced with black blood
screeching mothers wailing
whose wombs are scraped with force.

An endless succession of daily news reads
as a horror movie stuck on its reels
love reeking with pungent lies and stinking moments
leaving us feeling on the tip of a thousand needles and pins.

The incessant heap of your garbage lies
your lack of personal accountability,
your avaricious behavior is not the reflection of the people
you constantly try to divide.

Constant outpouring of disgust and despair
looming through the throbbing veins of this country
screaming, shouting *Blue Blue Blue*
enough to make our ancestors turn in their graves
you frequently play it down as a mere hullabaloo.

Your time is up and your throne is riddled with cracks
the pulverized dreams of those you thwarted
has come back to haunt you
with more than you can ask.

Stripping off your lies and ambiguities
this undulation of blue truth will soon
wash over this nation facing you as a threat.

Draining lies and perjury reeking in the high ranks
will leave you reflecting on your past four years
a scathing memory, you will deeply regret.

Winter Storm Moves Toward NYC

The blind white storm moves in with all its might and gust,
frothing river roars and bullies the waterfront with fading demarcation

as we see the water rising in far distant Manhattan
slightly fading before my eyes and its shimmering light, getting erased bit by bit

as the storm moves in. The continuous battering of my aching windows by the
boisterous gale trying to prove its existence through seething pain, a painful reminder.

My glass window sits like a denial between me and the vast river.
As I wonder; what angst, grief, or rage it carries under its calm waves.

But that was yesterday; today it is loud, as it lets out the bellowing cry hidden
between overlapping waves. It cries and howls like a black mother losing her son

countless times. I know there is more to this pain—
The pain that swells up the streets, pain seeping under the curbside

haunted memories forming the empty skeleton of the catacombs
that run through the porous veins of this city. This city moans

as the storm makes its way, tightening its grasp around its waist and choking
the last sliver of breath. The icy-cold veins get bluer with every passing minute.

Losing life with throbbing temples, life pulsating through the coarse hands of this city
finally let out its last cry. Hands thrown in despair, it genuflects on skinned knees.

Battered soul frenetically waiting for the storm to take it in fully, before the
next bullet is passed through the rib cage of yet another black body losing its life

to the trigger-hungry finger, laced with greed and white privilege;
rummaging and dismantling lives, like a winter storm.

A Living Fallacy

Yes, I choose,
choose not to be blindsided by the facts
printed in the reams of the newspaper daily
salient facts spoon-fed by national media
that every man has a voice.
A life created equally.

When an invisible virus guts this town like fish
outing the fears seeded in every living soul
revealing that breath of yours might be the last one
the truth forgotten for years,
has finally been brutally told.

It tells us that every breath is
indeed a privilege.
Life is not marked by
the color of skin, creed, and religion
blinded by false narratives for eons
breathing lies is the real false supposition.

The truth breathing its last
filling corrugated skies
thick with blood and smoke
caught like a deer in headlights
facing the end of a police gun
bodies piling up on streets
as protectors start to devour.

Fear culled in bones,
that you could be the next
definition of equality based on a false perspective
a constant war of narratives—

truth mercilessly hanged
in the hidden gallows of murky politics.

An invisible enemy that sits boisterously
on our couch laughs at us
claiming its territory
marking every corner we touch
teaches us that every man
indeed is created equal.

The virus teaches us equality
it does not spare the rich, or the downtrodden
and does not dispense rights
based on skin of your color.

It doesn't judge you how your tongue rolls
unlike where the country you live,
suddenly treats you like an infection
and selflessly disowns.

It took an invisible enemy of a hundred years
sprawling in the hidden corners of society
to reveal the unspoken truth
that it is the colorless breath, that counts after all.

A lesson etched in the folds of history
reiterated and retraced itself—
the virus doesn't close our eyes
doesn't blindfold me or you.

When nameless blood laces the sidewalk of this nation
the nation built on the fallacy
that all men are created equal.

Bullhorn

The streets were simmering with pain
laced with the blood of the innocent
as another black body faced the threat
of a loaded police gun
with death's gaping mouth open wide.

How frail is the thread of justice
when the protectors start to devour?
When the streets of your nations
are brimming with the wails of mothers unknown.

This was the sight seeded in every heart
when the neck of George Floyd
was choked for 9.29 minutes
begging for a shred of breath
with every minute that passed.

With the pandemic lurking
in every nook and corner of my city
a feeling of helplessness
ashen thoughts filled me.

With protest simmering in every iota of my being,
I took to my pen and started shaping the sadness in me.

I scratched the skin of the paper
to give a name to this burning feeling inside me
and drew posters for the march in my city
something that fills the eyes of my ten-year-old
with immense pride and a feeling of solidarity.

The road to justice is paved with good intentions
filled with its share of trials and tribulations.

Evil has no name and yet many—

Let us scrape the brackish taste of this violence
from the skin of our tongues
and the pain knotted in our spines
for endless generations.

Let us take our bullhorn
and wildly declare to this world
that *enough is enough*—
and piercing the ashen heart of these dark skies
a new day has boisterously begun.

Language of the Wound is Love

Language of the wound is love.
Loneliness leaning in the spaces between us
hearts knotted tightly as the wooden stump.

And all the atrocities carried in our gaping mouths
the provenance of hurt,
of surmountable desires;
of irreparable loneliness,
of sickled dreams,
splits the cold air like a scalpel
that bounds us, like the thin twig
keeping the broken stalks together.

Loneliness slowly seeps into the distance between us
and the color of the hurt gets darker
with every other shade
with every turn
with every twist knocking the tempest
and cutting close to the skin.

Skin grazed blood pooling in the scraped corners
here in this time and at this moment
nobody understands the semantics of my pain
a life left undefined.

Like a word spoken in a foreign world
I mispronounce your fear
and a new threat is born.

(III)

Every Pain Has a Story

Insane 'New' Normal

Like a blind cave
brittle rib cage hosting the infection
an unwanted guest—
the virus opens its mouth
and its glistening black teeth
in the dead of the night

devours everything
precious and beautiful,
cleaves life out of the soul
leaves you gasping
with bated breath and jarred mind

you are left alone
in a vacant mind
lying on your deathbed
reminiscing the day love embraced you
around a summer bonfire

now loneliness bounces off
sepia-tinged walls
death draped in pristine
white sheets folded
at the foot of this bed

scooping its share
masticating life
leaving you rotten
like an empty room with chipped-off walls
forgotten and waiting for its due

vacant mind begets explanation
in the hollowness of night
when the wheezing and choking
cleaves your soul
leaving you asunder

it rattles your mind
you struggle with the existential truth
as this insane '*new normal*' renders
dying alone, a new meaning.

A Condolence Call

Grief sits like a day-old soup in my kitchen unless anger stirs,
rattles, and boils it. Grief rises to the surface and chokes me—

I hear the loss of a mother. My friend's mother, over the phone
it's a condolence call yet I can't seem to join in his grief

Sudden loss disjoints your body, the pieces don't seem to fit anymore.
Body and language are extricable. Our tongue moves in a way

our body can't decipher in grief. I can't seem to form a legible sentence,
our conversation keeps coming back to the grocery, the loneliness of

being stuck in a condo looking over the lush green, deserted parks.
I don't want to bring back the conversation of the dead and dying.

The whole thread of conversation is about feeding the ones we love.
Loss is pouring through the thin sluices of this city. *Every damn day*.

Which starts again the same way it ended yesterday. Or was it tomorrow?
With sidewalks pitted with the bones of the dead, there is a new definition of normal.

I can't seem to fathom the desperation and anger in his voice of not being
able to visit his mother during her last times, the pain and the grief carry over

like a failing enjambment from one meaningless conversation
to another, till we ran out of small talk. The silence between

the pause takes the shape of unsaid condolence, as I slowly hang up the phone.
There is no defined language for grief. Lesson learned.

A Silent Witness

A silent witness to these passing days
as we hunker down in our little islands
seeking solace in unknown ways,
a veiled company in pixelated screens
when the cool pale glow
lights up the harsh pandemic nights.

This inexorable wait countings day by minute
when every second
split into   two
days and hours are doubled
closeness broods strange anxiety amongst us.

The angst and pain we fervently try
to hide behind our masked faces;
spills through our marred eyes
pitted with the fear of the unknown and unsaid.

Death comes in shades of yellow, red, and crimson
anointing everyone,
humanity has been reduced
to deathly tolls climbing on pages
dispensing death equally to the rich and the downtrodden.

Here we stand at the edge of humanity
looking for solace
in the wounds of the night sky,
a fallen star:
like a grieving mother
not letting go of her dead child.

Looking Outside

at empty streets and hallowed lanes stripped of
faces and laughter, cheers dying in fading noise.

There is more to this silence than the darkness stuck
in the black teeth of the night—

Thrumming of a lone harp wire, falling plain on my empty ears.
Rolling subways bouncing off the empty walls.

Silence screams the loudest, cleaving hunger in our souls.
Those pixelated appearances of gentle soft faces on the screen

are a metaphor for social company. A replacement for warm breaths
on the back of my neck for that phantom apricity.

Waves throbbing and breaking on empty shores return
half-hearted to places,

not baptized by the fleeting touch of soft palms,
and baby-fat legs dipped for mere excitement.

Giggles lost in the pulverized sands of the barren beach
call out for mercy. This deafening silence is no longer pristine and pure.

Social distancing is the sustenance we crave these days
as we now look with our parched eyes to foil the gaps in our sight.

A moment of isolation that we slowly brought upon ourselves
weaving this orphan moment, as the corrupt architect of this empty world.

Redemption

The pale blue glow has lit up
nooks and corners of our country
there is a strange closeness
in all the social distancing

we are alone, yet together, in this fight
the new normal crook their heads
from the slightly pixelated screens
mixed with the cold blue glow of pandemic nights

holding our disconnected thoughts in our connected minds
we move like a big ignoramus engine
toward the future
with anger, fear, and hope
mixed in equal proportions

surreal, dystopian ghosts of the future
living in futuristic shows
have suddenly taken a comfortable pose in
warm-lit corners of our living room

a boisterous unwanted presence—
dispensing justice with a blind eye
equally to the rich and the downtrodden

A new normal
laced with morphed and twisted reality
a bulging curve we are crazily
trying to flatten, yet failing fervently

news pitted with the death of the old and suffering
spilling from the rotten edges
of newspapers as we stand
here at the edge of humanity

swirling at the epicenter of this pandemic
calling out to our exalted gods in heaven
fervently trying to reason
which one of our seven deadly sins from the past
needs redemption?

Of Today and Tomorrow

How will you separate today and tomorrow
when everything will move blindly,
like a hamster's cage?

A big ball of unending yarn, with no beginning or end
separation of white and colored,
will not happen so swiftly as before
now it will be either infected or safe.

We live to bury our past—
wiping incessantly, tears streaming down
from burying our loved ones
alone in unmarked graves,
stashed like a garbage pile
in the refrigerated trucks,
our sorrows will carry their deep stench
through our thin veins forever
nothing will be lost to the wind.

The closeness, the tactile love
we all are desperately looking
will be long gone.
Now, every anxious eye will look
for the way out, a sterile haven,
anxiety churning a shade darker
with every passing moment.

Sorrow hidden behind those masks
will hide your pain forever.
Eyes, a window to your soul,

will now hide away your loneliness
as you stand six feet apart in a room
filled with loved ones.

Rolling nights with their jagged teeth
will continue to smirk.
The contagion sitting boisterously
hiding in the bushes
will be ready to spring at us
at any given moment,
while we will split between
the pain of burying our past
and grieving for the future
we once had.

Room with no name

The day stark white
numb and mute—
a tattered tarpaulin stretched
across thatched roof
barely meeting its purpose.

Static and buzzing incessantly
like a broken TV screen,
waiting for inspiration to strike
nights with its spiked teeth entering unannounced.

Unbidden

Moments, like a leftover bowl outside
overflows when left unattended.
I watch this intently with grief swirling
in my eyes.

Watching with unbroken attention
as seconds split into halves
days roll like a spindle
like a mindless manufactured journey.

As the sluice outside my house
carries the black grief my town gathers in
their empty hearts
into the dark belly of gutters
unknown and unacknowledged.

I sit here looking at the deaf sky
and mute air with its laughter stripped off.
I store my sorrow neatly between the folds

of my even pleated skirt
trying to give structure to my days.

Sitting at the edge of the window sill
breaking the skin of
raindrops from last night
my fingertips touch the windowpane
longing for company
in the room with no name.

Shelter in Poetry

We are hunkered down with this reality
plaguing us like a night with its serrated teeth
a nightmarish stairway to nowhere

slowly seeping as a black hole in our lives
stranded on our islands
cooped in the isolated corners of our little home
when the dystopian future
sits boisterously on my cushioned couch

mocking us as we look for a safe haven
in the flickering end-of-night light
seeking muse to dying quill in these trying times
solace to my reticent mind

as it struggles to find the meaning
unraveling in the cold corridors of life
unspooling life secrets
bringing every knackered fear out in the open

a burgeoned display of frenetic lies
trying to find solace in that sepia-tinged paper
as the days grew ashen
poetry holds the light in its cupped palms

a sane meaning to my discordant thoughts
screaming from every nook and corner
of my filled yet lonely room
as I try ardently
to find shelter in my poetry.

Unclaimed Freedom

The cerulean tinge peeking through barbed wires
a gaping hole, like an open, stretched calloused palm
seeking empathy in hunger, in pain—
color-tinged rays making their way
through the mishmash of thick wires

I squint my eyes to even the shades
even then, I can see the mesh obstructing my vision
there are too many restrictions these days
the invisible virus boisterously ruling our lives,
holding lien to our breaths
making us beg for the next one, a novel privilege

I want to rip apart this entrapment
pry open the obstructed view of the open skies
let the fraying ends come loose
shifting wings like a soaring eagle
in the vast cerulean skies
laced with mellifluous melody,
I want to taste freedom through my squinty eyes

I know this calling,
I can feel the warmth in my bones
sorrow draining from every iota of my existence
I take the clamps, cut the wires
one joint at a time
slowly but surely

Making way for my petite body
to pass through the thin gaps

of this corrugated mesh
and claim the freedom
which is truly mine.

Every Pain Has a Story

The nihilistic sky breaks open and rains on me. Its pain pried open and the monsoon always gives it a reason. I have a small wish cupped in my soft palms which bear witness to everything. Everything is real and forgotten. Yet it's buried like the pain of crumbled soil, breaking to give way to small saplings. We all are empty vessels of pain and anguish filled to the brim, ready to spill at any given moment. I see her passing in the empty hallways, eyes lowered and body shriveled. Ignorance can only exist for so long in a dimly lit corridor where we haven't had any human contact for months. Indifference and ignorance sit on the opposite spectrum of human emotions and I want her to tell that, *madly.* There have been countless such moments where hunger has risen clutching to the inner walls of my throat waiting to be spoken. We all wait for that big moment of revelation, that shiny orb of light shimmering around our bodies that will guide our soulmates toward us. We all believe in fantasies that want to exist in a surreal world. A world of bent clocks and melting moments. Pain is always interred in our memories and takes shape in our vivid dreams. How often have you dreamt about severed palms reaching out to you in fear and urgency in the deep folds of the night? This is not *Dali's* dream but reality unspooling secretly in the dimly lit corridors of my condominium. The flickering lights are like a fluttering dream existing in a different dimension. In this version of the dream, I want to cup her hands between my calloused palms and whisper gently in her ears that every pain has a story and a listener. Healing like the thrumming of a harp wire, it will reach its resonance if gently struck with perfect fingers.

(IV)

The Collective State of Disbelief

The Beautiful Death Around Us

Based on the invasive species, the lanternfly emerging in the summer of 2022 in the Eastern part of the United States

I have been taught by my granny to always help an animal in need.
Even an insect, a monarch with broken wings
fluttering in the shining mud,
shining bravely in the apricity of the city
stopping us in our tracks.

I hold it gently in the center of my tender palms, like an infant,
cuddling its existence with all my warmth
and tend to its broken wings, till it can fly.

One day, a small-breasted warbler crashed against the blinding windows
of my high-rise and fell on the balcony.
Death is a shining thing. It draws you in, like a pied piper.
A shining penny half-covered in a roll of hay.

I tend to its broken wings and wait feverishly for it to open its eyes.
Numerous tales of kindness and humility come back to me, rushing when
sometimes kindness
becomes a stranger to me.

These days are strange. The year is strange—
Death and the dying have been given a new name.
The normal has been anointed again.

And yet again, there is an invasive species, as beautiful as a dream in the thicket
of the night with its spotted wings and fiery abdomen.

A spotted lanternfly. And the message that it brings for us is; *"When you see it, kill it."*

What a terrible act of survival. It's either them or us. The existence is beautiful and yet so devastating.

Sometimes I feel how much kindness is left inside this withering soul of mine, which can kill a living being with all my might.

Fear Has No Shape, Yet Many

Fear has no shape and yet many. It seeps through the cracks of your ignorance and sits still in the crevices of your soul so deep with its thick tremulous still center.

Heavy as a stone, thick as an accusation. Fear of unknown hands in the dark, when the acknowledgment of identity seems more urgent than the violence itself.

Rage cracks you open like the fissure in the earth's skin, that travels as soft footsteps drowned by the heavy rain breaking it open, wherever it touches.

Fear, like unwanted burgeoning grief that straddles you for the rest of your life. You look for places to unload it. In the warm hands of loved ones, on the warm shoulders of those who with their gaping

hungry mouths are ready to devour your sorrows and endless grief. Fear like stillness in the breath of sparrows, nesting on the top of a thick bough of that mighty old oak tree that gets filled with

darkened gaze at the sight of death slithering near the roots, ready to devour its fledglings. Fear is counting the minutes to impending doom.

Fear, a hunger brimming in our core, spilling our guts for the world to see. Fear, turning our lives into a hollow deep mad menagerie.

Rage

If there could only be a way to contain the ringing in my ears.
The way the words bounce off the walls of my mind, as I press my palms against them

to stop this incessant sound, the echo of my words.
I can still feel the hallowed existence of everything around me.

A curdling ball of anxiety rolling down the stairs, the thump getting heavy with
every single step. Till it becomes a deafening sound that mutes every other and turns

it into a screech like that of a wild animal being skinned alive.
I can feel the dampness of blood curdling under my deft knees.

I hold myself still for this raging white death to pass through, for this deathly
moment to end, counting back the minutes, waiting for this incessant thrumming

to die down exactly the way my therapist instructed me. To wait patiently for the next wave
of blind anger to wash over me. Like a fleeting flash of heat coming off a burning kiln.

Needs and Wants

Countless lessons, and dreams that never reached their fruition
scars that I held as my armor
small moments in my life,
that served as my guiding beacon
these were moments of weakness—
of gratitude, of love, of belonging
hunger and acceptance.

Endless times I could count the teachings
on the soft tips of my bony fingers
recalling the night when the moon shines in its reverie
safely tucked in the cleavage of light and thunder.

These sublime crocheted memories
those corrugated desires—
an endless maze of needs and wants,
is the surreal path I traversed in life
a path carved with bone and sweat
lined with the grand stories of survival.

You will meet people who will make
you feel like a spring blossom
leaving you brimming and spilling with life.
And then there will be those
whose ashen sights will suck the nectar
leaving you seeded with strife.

Life is nothing but a dichotomy of emotions—
A rollercoaster of a ride.

I cannot teach you something that
you will finally learn in your own soft and nimble ways,

I always say this to my son;
we all have to make our own path
carve through the struggles deeply seeded in our souls,
and guide us through the thick ashen days.

I want you to remember this lesson
to stop looking at people as opportunities
and give them the deserving worth
they are striving so hard for.

Life will always be a struggle
look deep and connect with your heart—

There is more to this mysterious life
than your mere needs and wants.

Socially Acceptable

Where does your truth lie
in the vast spectrum of audacity?
Lingering between the shades of
falsehoods and sublimity.

Does the shade vary as the potency of truth gets diluted?
As the concentration of lies dissolves,
it churns a new mixture
a new potency—

A tad bit stronger than the previous lie
which has been gulped unanimously
/Not so jarring/
soothing throats of the naysayers
standing on the brim.

Carefully selecting shades of truth
picking the right shades,
that can sit comfortably
in their long craning necks.

Before they spat out the version
which is a little tart
a truth not so sweet—
but socially acceptable.

The Perfect Solution

The muted rumblings of my soul
have broken the sky into two
one part of it cries and another
turns into a puddle on the pavement.

It stores the reflection of my dreams
till a stone breaks its skin
and shatters its identity.

How far can you see inside a heart
when it is muddled with hate,
fear, and anxiety?

How far can we really see?

The setting sun leaves an ochre shade
a burnished reflection;
on everything around me.

It seems we are on fire
even on the coldest of the nights
you fail to see the passion simmering in me.

Sound cannot travel in a vacuum
it needs a medium for itself to carry
the fear of the unknown
of hate and anxiety,
of skin color not known to us
poisoning minds of the free.

See, I have to scream loud
for all caged minds to hear me.
Diversity is not a curse
it's the only cure for our ailing humanity.

Exceptional

Buried under the dearth of pain
lies, suffering, hatred, and loss
we humans as a species
continue to survive.

Every day we overcome
the fear of discrimination,
misogyny,
clash of religions, morals, and values,
and still, we continue to survive.

All the bloodthirst and the violent
numbness that the soul goes through
a dried trail of tears and hopeless dim humanity
and still, we continue to survive.

Living under the false pretense
surrounded by all the hatred
cheating and betrayal;
love being lost in the rampant chaos
and still, we continue to survive.

Compassion and threadbare empathy
lose all their meaning
false hopes and lip sympathy
continue to reign
and still, we continue to survive.

Riding the food chain
and dominating the world
threatening and corrupting nature
sucking nature till it dries up
and still, we continue to survive
we, humans.
Aren't we exceptional?

A False Arrangement

How old is your body?
How old do you feel?
Ricocheting memories
through sepia-tinged walls.

Unscarred and unscathed recollections
lodged into your throat
cutting and grazing you slowly;
every time you try to push
and gulp it down a little more.

Those tentacles of the past have
clawed deeply into your soul
holding onto you, like a blood-sucking parasite
they breathe. They thrive on your fear.

Those callous hands remind you
of those sharp convictions cutting through your skin
those age-old bunions, swelling through time.

Peeling off the pellicle of your fingers
like the acid falling on your yellow skin
suppurating with welts and blisters.

They always forget only your skin has a color
that sets you apart
your soul is colorless. *No taste and no odor,*
like water.

It will seamlessly take the shape of the next vessel
it will pour into you;
while you are busy arranging
the vases in the order of their color.

Smokescreen

Clouds hovering over this city finally fell
they gave in—
every face splashed
with tears of the sky.

Nobody can't really tell
if sadness exists only in the eyes.
Every face is more dejected than the other,
loneliness etched in wrinkles
seeping between spaces
of an unclutched palm
reaching out, longing for acceptance.

Agony stringing together this city
made of ivory dreams,
thriving on undulating spines
cowering under the pain
of each passing day, an ache filling the spaces
between ribs thick with greed.

Those twin skyscrapers once piercing
the crimson bosom of open skies
where every day begins with
a promise waiting to be kept
now a nightmarish routine—
a horror movie stuck on its reels.

With mouth agape, eyes mocking
revered reality; salted with broken desires
sorrow leans between the spaces,
filling the gaps left by life
for the crouched souls on a crowded subway.

Saving is a Grace Bestowed by the Almighty

in a world where we live
every other breath is laced and mixed
with fear and anxiety in equal proportion.

A world suffused with wishes
broken desires and hushed whispers;
a world doused with frenzy and mayhem
dreams frayed at the ends,
bursting apart at the seams
brittle hopes failing, as a tourniquet for my bleeding self.

A convoluted mind
boisterous too at times—
leading everyone into a frenzy and mayhem
a blind bagpiper leading the country
in such visceral times.

A poem with frail breaths
gasping and scratching the innards of words
frantically looking for its sustenance.
A poem with its tremulous still center
heavy as a stone—
thick as an accusation,
can't seem to absolve our sins.

Poetry in times like these
affords us no such luxury
as the warmth of our soft words
falling endlessly in the insides of a hungry mouth.
A mere drop in the vast barren chest of parched lands.

My juxtaposed mind unspooling the puzzle quietly
looking out the broken window frame
smiling alone, lighting up my crow's feet
thinking how many of the sparrows
lining my courtyard will I save this summer
with my half-broken cup, held by frail hands.

The Collective State of Disbelief

How mad and hopeful is the hunger
seeded in the heart of Cormorant diving
from vast heights, risking the possibility
of getting blinded by the speed of their dives.

Hunger precedes the need for existing.

That's how boisterously it wilts in your soul.
It holds the lien to your heart and you become
a being of no sane reason, driven entirely by pleasure,
driven by ecstasy, driven by hunger and its feverish needs.

You are played like a sin in the hands
of those whom you trust and are left
in a state of prolonged emptiness.

This perplexing state of existence
has pushed me toward the edge, every time
but despite this, I turn around, driven by my hunger
that says to me aloud;

Stay here, Look, we all are dying
living in a collective state of disbelief.

(V)
Brotherhood

To Begin Something, Something Needs to End

Walking on the curving path of the waterfront for an early morning walk greeted by smiling faces behind masks, smiling through their eyes.

Yes, I know they are. The simple beauty of nature cannot be hidden for long, as the small saplings and dainty vines make their way through the cracked pavement, growing and fighting,

for sustenance and a share of the sun's apricity. This is a moment of pause and a moment to act. A moment where even though we are hunkered down with our version of realities,

we share collected grief, the collective truth that makes us human. That teaches us nature knows its ways to heal. *She leads and we follow* and there is no other way for us beings.

Trying to outsmart nature has put us back in the starting position. We realize we live at the mercy of nature, at the mercy of invisible things, heavily and boisterously felt in our lives.

We know this is not the end, but the beginning of something so profound—This moment of pause, this moment of introspection in our feeble lives

that needs us to find our way through this maze while observing the divine glow of fireflies crowding our backyards on dark summer nights, or the yellow-breasted warbler

waking me up in the wee hours of the morning, or the stars that appear closer to us these days. The air feels more scented. A face, a hand, or a touch matters more in this virtual world.

That we owe our lives to Mother Earth, who blesses us with her love but will also take it all back in the blink of an eye. To know that this is not the end

but the beautiful beginning of something that has been ignored for so long; Like a poem waiting to be read aloud.

Simple Pleasures

A desire so pure
so serene,
like a tender squeal of a newborn—
soft faint whispers of prayers
from nearby temples
hunger in your voice travels
farther than the longing for a stuffed belly

a belly full of desires—
of compounding hunger,
this hunger births beauty
a fertile ground,
a sprouting seed, for an artistic desire

Hunger strips away the deception
leaves you clean,
stripped of vices
I feel complete, to the sound of you reading your favorite poem
sacred as a muezzin call to prayer

The words warm up spaces between us
in the middle of the night
as loneliness leans onto them

Simple pleasures are the deepest.
The contentment of getting fed by mother
that ambrosial meal;
those lumps of food
salvation in each morsel.

A tasteful memory deeply seeded in my heart
that longs for more,
more than a belly full of desire—
more than the pleasure of entwined bodies

This body is built on desires
carved on the jagged edge of mounting wishes
an endless succession—
of simple pleasures.

Trails of Kindness

I count the years as I walk past the trees lining my courtyard.
Counting them one by one neatly on my supple fingers.

The mighty oak has weathered worse and still nests
sparrows. The jasmine tree, whose flower-laden shoots

smile through their fragrant arms, waves me goodbyes.
Their warm presence deeply carried by northern winds.

Even with a slight opening in my kitchen window, they can make their
presence felt.
What more to this life, than to count joys and blessings in the crawling lines

of my mint plant that is growing and spilling joys in all directions. The new
tender leaves of basil, twinkling and shining through the sliver of sunlight.

Warm supple hands of my succulents, holding water as kindness in their
thick leaves, remind me of the frail hands of my granny combing my hair and
making trails of kindness.

Reminding me always that kindness is a necessary gesture of acceptance.
Like the puny sapling, breaking through the crumbling earth

as it finds hope and grows through pain.

On Listening to Jericho Brown

Writing with urgency: an aching desire
a rising hunger in a parched throat

when the craft and empathy are inseparable—
seething feeling resonating with tenderness and sorrow

a zoetic language: a soft growl turning into a wail.
haunting that resonates, leaving me like a thrumming harp wire

such is the riveting effect of his words
an unraveling of his intricate mind—

a mind with aching desire, a nuanced understanding
of the turmoil that surrounds and is within us

a hunger he experiences
while writing a truth that readily burns

a hunger that clings to my ribs, as thick as greed,
and never leaves. A longing, a desire

for the unnamed passions in my soul
a cleaving opening of my transgressions

and I face the proximity of my desires
like standing next to a burning kiln

how it warms me up, the unstoppable—
whirling into the void. Swallowed like a dream

reaching the end of the abyss,
where everything seems so surreal

reminds me of the moment when it all began
as I stand in admiration. Speechless.

The Uprising

The lost rhetoric in those verses
when the words drop their veils
and meaning is shaved off from
each side of the numbing silence

those resonating words have
been loitering around without a cause
orphaned in their own existence
lost without a doubt

you try to drape them
give meaning to them,
through your false pretense and your ambiguities
but the valiant truth will stand tall
stare in your face
with its unfrazzled glow
shimmering and shining

like a thousand summer suns,
till your skin is turned yellow
your incongruence aberrant thoughts
your ambivalence,
will die a painful death

a life full of duality
your facade will be
pulverized and shattered
into a million pieces,
when the truth will
rise with all its nudity.

A Bridge Needs to be Built

Not every thought stirs me up. Not every flicker brightens my heart
it takes a thousand steps in my heart, to take one little step toward you.

Not every morning brightens my soul, not every rain washes my sins.
I have knelt on so many pews seeking absolution.

Not every prayer absolves my sins. Not every scar sings songs of my glory.
Not every wrinkle is chiseled with experience.

I'm a fleck of mortality riding the winds of time.
Not every moment of history carves me.

Not every sin I commit defines me. Not every blank space in my heart can be filled.
Not every thought of mine can be aligned.

But every day in me, I find myself a bridge that needs to be built.
A dark corner that needs to be lit.

Rise

Rise,
rise above the opinionated heads
on stooping shoulders of demised desires
on your sturdy legs or stilts
but rise and become the voice of the unspoken
war cry of the mute
hoarse whispers of the fallen
in the crevice of night.

Rise,
when their tongue is sliced and gutted out
and vultures are feeding on their dead entrails.
Don't be a mute spectator
they will speak through you
like an apparition,
like a ghost in the machine,
and will beg you to stay.
Be a *Massiah*
ready to be burned at the stake.

Rise,
enrage their souls
buried deep in their shame
your tongue born out of fire
raising hair at the back of their neck
speaking in an unborn tongue;
like a catalyst for a revolution,
you give them a mission
a purpose,

a reason for their crestfallen souls,
a tourniquet for their bleeding wounds,
a moment to survive,
a shiny glimpse of the future.

Rise,
bedazzle them
rise like Phoenix
out of thin air
devour the stench of pointy accusations.

Rise up to see a new dawn
like the hope,
neatly tucked in the crevices
of the unbroken seed.

Act Beautifully

If only we could truly realize the consequences of our actions
preached endless times but still failed to get the real essence.

If only we could hear the sounds of souls and withering hearts
that we mercilessly shatter as we continue to live.

We live in a world laced with desire and hunger
of needs and wants, of acceptance and rejection.

While we continue to pave our path to success no matter if it is laced
and seeped with the blood of many —we continue to live, we continue to
exist.

We look for monsters in others failing to turn the mirror toward us
the faint remembrance of who we truly are.

Kindness that should flow through our veins
symphony of love that we all should syncopate to.

I'm lost here in translation. Like the tattered book forgotten
to be picked from the dusty shelf, old and forgotten, waiting for
kindness that never returns.

And yet, here I am still waiting for mindless conversations
in this room to end slithering from one selfish ear to another.

Waiting for a sliver of golden silence. They say silence has its own language
a lost art that needs an interpretation.

To have that stillness that lies in the knotted legs of a meditative monk
or the mellifluous beauty of a swirling dervish.

To know that we all need to listen, not *hear*.
Listen to the heartbeats that tell us the simple truth.

To act beautifully, to find the plinth of our existence.
To find the soul of the poem open for interpretation.

Brotherhood

"We must live together as brothers or perish together as fools."
—Martin Luther King Jr.

We are all broken, crumbled
rounded again
made from the same clay
caked and baked in the same
unforgiving oven.

We all have cracks in us
from where the light gets in—
frayed at the border
pulling apart at the seams,
peeling off and breaking down
into pieces of our miseries.

We are all the same
living under the same
ashen cloudless sky
and blue moon in its reverie.

Breathing the same air
swooning over the same
melody of the soul
crooning our necks
to the same broken chords
in unison, we roll.

We all are the same
laughing and cracking up
with welled-up eyes
and bruises we endure.

Getting stabbed by the same knife
and bloodied by the same bullet
cast creed or religion
doesn't seem to discriminate
or beg to differ.

We are all the same
same heartbeats
sliced and splintered into a million pieces,
and the same God we worship
holding books with different verses.

We all are the same from within
laughing at our scars
with abject profundity.

We are brothers and sisters
together we shall live.

Acknowledgments

Grateful acknowledgment to the editors of the following journals and anthologies in which some of these poems, or earlier versions of them, first appeared.

"Life in Quarantine" Project, Center for Spatial and Textual Analysis (CESTA), Stanford University:
"A Condolence Call"
"Looking Outside"
"Insane *New* Normal"
"Shelter in Poetry"

2022 First Place Winner Broadside Poetry Contest, San Gabriel Valley Festival:
"Saving is a Grace Bestowed by the Almighty"

Aired on WNYC Studio as part of National Poetry Month 2022/ Boundless Anthology 2021, FlowerSong Press:
"Deciphering the Madness"

New York Public Library (NYPL) ezine Vol 5:
"To Begin Something, Something Needs to End"

New York Public Library (NYPL) ezine Vol 6:
"Needs and Wants"

National League of American Pen Women "The Pen Women" and Walk_Bye, An International Public Exhibit:
"Trails of Kindness"

Memory House Magazine, University of Chicago Press:
"My Bones Rattle with Crimson Rage"

2022 National Beat Poetry Foundation Anthology:
"My Identity as a First Generation Immigrant"

2023 National Beat Poetry Foundation Anthology:
"Ghost In a Different Dimension"

2024 National Beat Poetry Foundation Anthology:
"Act Beautifully"

2022 BrownStone Poets Anthology, Nominated for the Pushcart:
"Poem and Its Hunger"

World Inkers Publications, Nominated for Best of the Net:
"The Uprising"

2023 Boundless Anthology, FlowerSong Press:
"Provenance of My Rage"

Doves Born of Flames Anthology, Lever Press,
Middlebury Institute of International Studies:
"Planting Seeds in a Detention Center"

Visual Verse, London/Berlin Online Journal/
New Castle Center for the Literary Arts:
"Deserted"

"The Kali Project" Anthology, Indie Blue Publishing Press/
Journal of Commonwealth Literature, 2022:
"Just Another Day, Just Another Rape"

Black Fire This Time, Vol 2, Willow Books:
"Topography of a Wound"

2023 Brownstone Poets Anthology:
"Love is Nothing but an Elegy for Acceptance"

2024 Calling All Poets 25th Anniversary Anthology:
"The Beautiful Death Around Us"

North of Oxford Press:
"Unclaimed Freedom"
"Living Fallacy"

Rising Phoenix Review:
"On Listening to Jericho Brown"

Oddball Magazine:
"House of Our Forgotten Past"

The Brown Critique, Brown Critique Books:
"Branded"

Moonstone Arts Press, Moonstone Arts Center:
"Time's Up"
"Socially Acceptable"

Anthology "Re-Imagine America", Vagabond Press:
"Bullhorn"

American Writers Review:
"A Silent Witness"

Willowdown Books:
"Redemption"

Anthology "Home", SETU Publications:
"I Have Called Many Places Home"
"A Bridge Needs to be Built"

Anthology "The Arcade of the Scribes", Rogue Scholars Press:
"Permanence"

Anthology "Pandemic", Culture Cult Press:
"Of Today and Tomorrow"

Alien Buddha Press:
"Room with No Name"

Muddy Poetry Review:
"A False Arrangement"

Anthology "Twin Towers", Local Gems Press:
"Smokescreen"

Madras Courier:
"Simple Pleasures"

Fevers of the Mind Press:
"Brotherhood"

Al-Khemia Poetica, National Women's Month:
"Rise"

Also by Megha Sood

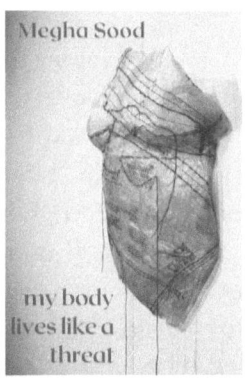

My Body Lives Like a Threat
by Flower Song Press, 2022

First Place Winner, Contemporary Poetry Category
2024 The BookFest Awards

Semi-finalist for the 2023 Housatonic Book Awards
Western Connecticut State University's MFA

Finalist, Poetry Category
"2022 Best Book Awards" by American Book Fest

Semi-finalist for the 2022 "Sherly Holden Helben" Grant
National League of American Pen Women NLAPW

Finalist, Poetry Category
2022 National Indie Excellence Book Awards

Honorable Mention
2022 New York Book Festival

Official Selection
2022 Indo-American Arts Council Literary Festival, Callum Gallery, NY

About the Author

Megha Sood(She/Her) is an award-winning Asian-American author, poet, editor, curator, and literary activist from New Jersey. She earned her Postgraduate Degree in Computer Application (M.C.A)and Bachelors in Computer Sciences (B.Sc.) from India. Her literary partnership "Life in Quarantine" with Stanford University has been presented at the Open Education Global Forum 2020 and received mention in the *Stanford Daily* newspaper. Her works have been supported by the National League of American Pen Women, VONA, Kundiman, Dodge Foundation, and Martha Vineyard Creative Writing Institute.

Her four poetry collections include the award-winning *My Body Lives Like a Threat* (FlowerSong Press, 2022) and *My Body is not an Apology* (Finishing Line Press, 2021). She was inducted as an honored listee for the 125-year-old Marquis Who's Who. A 2020 National Level Winner for the Poetry Matters Project, and a Four-Time State Level Winner for the NAMI NJ Dara Axelrod Poetry Award. Recipient of "Certificate of Excellence" from Mayor Stephen Fulop, Jersey City. Member of National League of American Pen Women (NLAPW), The Artists Forum (USA), ArtPride (NJ), and United Nations Association-US Chapter. She has also been chosen as a featured poet for the 2024 Dodge Poetry Festival.

Her widely anthologized poems, essays, and other works discuss her experience as a first-generation immigrant and woman of color. Her 900+ works have been widely featured in print, online journals, public exhibits, and anthologies including the Poetry Society of New York, *MS Magazine*, NYPL, *Pen Magazine* by American Pen Women, *Journal of NJ Poets, Dime Show Review, Panoplyzine*, PBS *American Portrait*, NPR, WNYC Studio, etc., and numerous universities including Stanford University, John Hopkins, Howard University, George Mason, Temple University, etc. Her poem "Deciphering the Madness" was also broadcast on WNYC-Studio Morning Edition as part of National Poetry Month in April 2022.

Her co-edited anthology "The Medusa Project" and other works have been selected to be sent to the moon in 2025 in two separate rocket missions as part of the historical LunarCodex Project in collaboration with NASA/SpaceX. She lives in New Jersey with her husband and her 14-year-old son. Find her at https://linktr.ee/meghasood.

FLOWERSONG
PRESS

**FlowerSong Press nurtures essential verse
from, about, and throughout the borderlands.
Literary. Lyrical. Boundless.**

Sign up for announcements about
new and upcoming titles at:

www.flowersongpress.com

www.ingramcontent.com/pod-product-compliance
Lightning Source LLC
Chambersburg PA
CBHW020421130626
46549CB00006B/2684